P9-DCR-509

WITHDRAWN
Speedway Public Library

MILTON
AND HIS WORLD

A pocket Bible which belonged to Oliver Cromwell. His signature is on the fly-leaf of this edition of 1658—the year of his death.

Cheapside was an area with which Milton would have been familiar, as many of the houses in which he lived were situated near this bustling commercial district. This view of Cheapside in 1638 shows the procession of Marie de Medici entering London on a state visit to Charles I and Henrietta Maria, her son-in-law and daughter. The large cross is one of the Eleanor Crosses erected by Edward I in 1290 to mark the resting-places of his wife's funeral cortège on the journey from Lincoln to burial in Westminster.

MILTON
AND HIS WORLD

C. V. WEDGWOOD

New York   HENRY Z. WALCK, INC.

First American edition, 1969

Acknowledgements

THE Publishers wish to thank the following for permission to reproduce photographs of which they hold the copyright. The numbers in brackets refer to the pages on which they appear: The London Museum [1, 2, 8, 10 (lower), 11, 14 (upper and lower left), 17 (upper), 24, 30, 31, 35, 42 (upper), 43, 45 (right), 47 (lower)]; National Portrait Gallery [5, 13, 14 (right), 38 (left), 41, 42 (lower)]; The Guildhall Library [6, 7, 17 (lower), 45 (left)]; Geffrye Museum and Mr. L. Taylor [9]; National Monuments Record [10]; the Burrell Collection, Glasgow Art Gallery and Museum [12]; Ministry of Public Building and Works [15, 23, 25]; Archives Department, London Borough of Hammersmith Public Libraries [16]; The Library, Edinburgh University [18, 19, 46 (upper), 47 (upper)]; Mansell Collection [20, 26, 28, 34, 39 (lower)]; Crown-copyright, The Science Museum, London [21, 22, 40 (lower)]; Radio Times Hulton Picture Library [27, 29, 48 (lower)]; City Art Gallery, Manchester [31 (left)]; the Controller of H. M. Stationery Office for facsimiles of Crown-copyright records, SP 23/101/ p. 925, and SP 18/37, no. 37, in the Public Record Office [32, 39 (upper)]; British Museum [33, 36]; National Maritime Museum [37, 38 (right)]; Guildhall Museum [40 (left), 46 (left)]; *A History of the British Fire Service* by G. V. Blackstone, published by Routledge & Kegan Paul Ltd. [44]; Princeton University Library [48]

Standard Book Number: 8098-3082-5

Library of Congress Catalog Card Number: 70–82682

COPYRIGHT © 1969 C. V. WEDGWOOD

DESIGN AND PRODUCTION © 1969 LUTTERWORTH PRESS

Printed in Great Britain

John Milton (1608–1674)
in his early twenties.

`J`OHN MILTON was born early in the morning on Friday, December 9, 1608, in Bread Street, London. His father was a scrivener, a profession which combined in a small way the functions of a notary and a banker. John Milton senior, had a thriving business and was well known in the City of London, but he was not a Londoner born. His father was an Oxfordshire yeoman. The poet thus combined in his inheritance the old agricultural England of corn, pasture and sheepfold with the new urban England of expanding commerce and finance with its heart in the City of London.

The poet's yeoman grandfather, like many countryfolk in the midlands, was true to the Old Religion (Roman Catholicism), but his father had become a Protestant. This had caused an irreparable quarrel between them. Thus the young Milton knew, among his nearest kindred, the bitter religious differences which divided his countrymen. He was himself to play a part in the struggle between the Anglican Church and its Puritan critics which reached an explosive climax in the Civil War of 1642.

5

Milton's parents were not young when he was born. His father was about forty-six, his mother in her thirties. Their only surviving child hitherto was a daughter, so that the late-born eldest son was from the first the object of their devotion. Some years later the family was completed by the birth of a younger boy, Christopher; but the gifted and intellectually precocious John remained the favourite.

'His home was the typical household of a respectable citizen—somewhat crowded by modern standards, since it housed not only the family but their servants and apprentices, and his father also conducted his business from it. Milton's mother, for her part, would see to the housekeeping and watch over her kitchen, larder and laundry as well as her nursery. Almost certainly, since Milton's father took his religion seriously, there would be family prayers every day. On Sunday the household would attend the parish church at least once, and frequently twice. But the scrivener had some more genial interests. He sang, he composed music; he had even contributed a piece of his own composition to one of the numerous collections of songs published in the later years of Queen Elizabeth I. The young Milton grew up to take deep pleasure in making music.

His father sent him to London's most famous school, St. Paul's, in the shadow of the lofty Gothic cathedral. It was only a few minutes' walk from his home, through cobbled streets between timber houses whose overhanging upper storeys almost shut out the day light.' On his way, the studious boy must often have paused to scan the tempting wares displayed by the booksellers who congregated round St. Paul's.

These etchings give us an idea of what London streets looked like in Milton's time. The costumes are late eighteenth-century, as these drawings were executed for the purpose of putting on record buildings which had survived the Great Fire, but which were then due to be demolished.

At school he pursued his studies with passion. He learnt Latin, Greek and Hebrew. Since modern languages were not then part of the curriculum, he studied French and Italian out of school hours. His father, unencumbered by modern theories about fresh air, exercise and sound sleep, indulged him to the full in his zeal for learning. Night after night he was allowed to sit up reading until twelve o'clock with a yawning maid-servant in attendance and expensive candles burning. As school in the seventeenth century began at seven in winter and six in summer the growing boy had, by modern standards, far too little sleep. Yet his health does not seem to have been affected, and the often repeated theory that too much reading by candlelight irreparably weakened his eyes is no longer held to be true.

Milton enjoyed and profited by his years at St. Paul's. He made several lasting friendships with boys who shared his tastes, chief among them Charles Diodati, son of an Italian Protestant refugee who had become a famous London physician. For nearly twenty years Diodati was to be the confidant with whom Milton discussed his ambitions, his hopes and his troubles. But in spite of his own evidently successful school-days, he was in later life to condemn in the strongest terms the teaching given to English schoolboys. In his tractate *Of Education* he would complain of the way in which they were tormented over small points of Latin grammar and made to waste their time composing their own bad Latin instead of reading and enjoying the works of the great masters.

An early nineteenth-century engraving of St. Paul's School, with Christopher Wren's St. Paul's Cathedral on the right. The school was gutted during the Great Fire but re-built immediately afterwards to the same design as the original, consisting of a low central building which housed the school-rooms and two taller structures on either side in which the masters lived.

Gothic St. Paul's Cathedral, which Milton would have passed daily on his way to and from school. The tower had once borne a 493-foot steeple, but this was destroyed by lightning in 1561. This engraving shows the new West Front, designed by the famous architect, Inigo Jones, which was not erected until after Milton's schooldays were over. The cathedral was not used for church services in Cromwell's time, and cheap stalls and shops were set up beneath the portico.

In spite of his strictures on the system, his own career showed that, with a good teacher, the seventeenth-century school could provide an intelligent pupil with a master key to the philosophy of Greece, the practical wisdom of Rome and the magical poetry of both. On the other hand, a boy with a bent for mathematics or science could get nothing from such education. The teaching of these subjects had not yet reached the schools, and for the difficult or backward child the long hours, tiresome and exacting lessons and harsh discipline were unalleviated torment.

By the time he was fifteen Milton had shown his talent for poetry by re-casting some of the Psalms in English verse. He cultivated his Latin style no less assiduously. The ability to write Latin might be useless to the average schoolboy, but it was essential to a man of learning who wished to communicate his thoughts to a wide audience. Latin was the international language not only of diplomacy but in every branch of learning. English was not then spoken outside England, and very few English books were translated into other languages. Italian, Spanish, French and Dutch were all more

8

widely spoken. Francis Bacon composed his most important works in Latin. William Harvey, who was lecturing in English on the circulation of the blood at the College of Physicians all through Milton's childhood, put his great discovery into Latin when he issued it to the world in 1628 from a press not in London but in Frankfurt.

Thus John Milton studied to write Latin as the best means of intellectual communication with the leading thinkers and scholars of all nations, whose ranks he was one day ambitious to join. But he also wanted to be an English poet. Even if educated foreigners thought little of the language, the English themselves were fully aware of its beauty and believed that they could and would create a great literature. Milton grew up in a great epoch of literature; he grew up in London where the living eloquence of John Donne was to be heard in the pulpit and the living poetry of Shakespeare, John Webster and Ben Jonson vibrated in the theatres. He read and admired—as all his contemporaries did—the richly wrought poems of Edmund Spenser. English poets had indeed already proved to their countrymen how subtle, varied and melodious an instrument they had at their command—an instrument no whit inferior to the great classical tongues, or to the musical Italian which still dominated European taste.

Milton had been brought up in a God-directed, God-fearing household. He treated his gifts seriously, looking upon his life and his career as something dedicated to God and the service of his country. This was as true of poetry as of theology or philosophy. When still quite young he was to write of the way in which a poet should strive to live worthily. He ought "himself to be a true poem, that is a composition and pattern of the best and honourablest things, not presuming to sing high praises of heroic men or famous cities unless he have in himself the experience and the practice of all that which is praiseworthy".

A museum reconstruction of how a room in a mid-seventeenth-century private house might have looked. The rooms were lit by candles and rushlights, and heated by log or coal fires supported on fire dogs.

MILTON WAS seventeen when he left St. Paul's for Christ's College, Cambridge. Here his handsome, sensitive face, silky curls and fastidious manners earned him the nickname of "the Lady". His Cambridge career was chequered by disagreements with an unsympathetic tutor but he completed his studies successfully with a Master's degree in 1632. Although he owed much to the seven years he spent at Cambridge, he was outspokenly critical of university teaching. He rightly condemned the narrowness both of learning and method then prevalent in both the English universities. What could the average young man make of it all? After years at school wrestling with trivial points of grammar, he came up to the university to be immediately confronted "with the most intellective abstractions of logic and metaphysics". As for the tutors, they simply abandoned their hapless pupils to be "tossed and turmoiled with their unbalasted wits in fathomless and unquiet deeps of controversy". Small wonder that many quitted the university with an ineradicable hatred of learning.

In a Latin oration at the close of his university career Milton eloquently expressed his own belief in a more imaginative and comprehensive education. His opinion echoed the ideas of the best minds of his age—ideas which were not yet embodied in any university teaching. New horizons, both intellectual and material, had been opened up by the explorations and discoveries of the previous century. Scientific inquiry into the nature of the universe and of man—astronomy, medicine, and the related natural sciences—attracted the best intellects of Europe. The art of printing had made possible the wide propagation of new knowledge to an ever-widening public. The Renaissance ideal of education, many-sided, profound and comprehensive, seemed to be within reach. No one had yet realized that the knowledge available would soon grow far too great for a single intellect to absorb. It was still possible in Milton's time to cultivate the

10

arts and the sciences with equal profundity and success. The age of specialization lay in the future.

At the university Milton had begun his career as an English poet. In the year that he went to Christ's College he wrote the elegy *On the Death of a Fair Infant*—a youthful, mannered exercise intended to console his married sister Anne who had suffered a bereavement all too common at that time. In 1629, when he was twenty-one, came his first great poem, the hymn *On the Morning of Christ's Nativity*. This majestic work, rich alike in imagery and in verbal music, calls up a vision of the false gods of Egypt, Carthage, Greece and Rome fleeing before the "heaven born Child" in the manger.

After this achievement Milton was well enough known among the clever young men at the university to be asked to contribute a commendatory sonnet to the second folio edition of Shakespeare's plays. He wrote the beautiful but rather stilted lines beginning:

> What needs my Shakespeare for his honour'd Bones,
> The labour of an age in piled Stones . . .

He did truly admire Shakespeare, he, who in the ultimate perspective of time was to stand second to him (although a long way second); yet the division of temperament between the two men is brought out in every line Milton wrote about him. What he admired in Shakespeare was the grace, the natural flow, the "easy numbers", the "woodnotes wild". To him Shakespeare was a natural force, a spring of poetry as simple and refreshing as a spring of water in some sweet pastoral dell. He himself, a man of books and "slow endeavouring art", was not temperamentally fitted to understand the infinite wisdom of Shakespeare which had so little to do with learning and so much to do with the common day-to-day experience of living.

The summer vacation of 1631 brought forth *L'Allegro* and *Il Penseroso*, an exquisite pair of pastoral pictures in which the muses, nymphs and goddesses of his classical learning mingle naturally with the meadows and streams, cities, villages and college chapels of his native land:

> Straight mine eye hath caught new pleasures
> Whilst the landscape round it measures,
> Russet lawns and fallows gray,
> Where the nibbling flocks do stray,
> Mountains on whose barren breast
> The labouring clouds do often rest:
> Meadows trim with daisies pied,
> Shallow brooks and rivers wide . . .

11

There was nothing of the Puritan about either of these graceful poems—very much the contrary. In *Il Penseroso* Milton describes with sensuous delight the splendour of stained glass and organ music:

> But let my due feet never fail,
> To walk the studious Cloisters pale,
> And love the high embowed Roof,
> With antick Pillars massy proof,
> And storied Windows richly dight,
> Casting a dim religious light.
> There let the pealing Organ blow,
> To the full-voiced Quire below,
> In Service high and Anthems clear,
> As may with sweetness, through mine ear,
> Dissolve me into ecstasies,
> And bring all Heaven before mine eyes . . .

Was he thinking of some rapt hour in King's College Chapel?

At Cambridge he was still contemplating the Church as a career. It was the obvious choice for a gifted intellectual, and his loving parents, especially his father, had certainly foreseen a career in the ministry for their wonderful son. But soon after leaving the university he decided not to be ordained. His reasons were not far to seek. He said himself that he had been shocked by the frivolous and even unseemly conduct of many of his young contemporaries at Cambridge who were studying for the ministry. He was probably also repelled by witnessing much unworthy scheming for patronage and preferment. The Anglican Church was in grave economic difficulties, and even those who entered the Church with a true sense of vocation could be easily corrupted by the need to please a powerful patron or to secure a comfortable benefice.

He may also have come into contact with the Puritan groups at Cambridge which congregated in the Colleges of Sidney Sussex and Emanuel, post-Reformation foundations with a rigidly Protestant tradition. He was certainly disturbed by such things as the dismissal by the King of the Professor of Ancient History for his allegedly subversive lectures on the Roman Republic. Royal authority grazed him much more nearly when a close personal friend of his, Alexander Gill, son of the high master of Saint Paul's, got into serious trouble for having expressed, at a private gathering, his joy at the murder of the King's favourite, the hated Duke of Buckingham. Young Gill was sentenced to pay a heavy fine, to stand in the pillory and to lose both his ears. The ferocious sentence was never in fact carried out, but neither Gill nor his friends were likely to forget the injustice of the prosecution. Milton certainly longed for greater

Two ornate seventeenth-century chairs which illustrate the change in styles between the periods of Charles I and Charles II. (Above) A tall-backed, cane-seated chair of about 1680, elaborately carved in walnut, a wood which became fashionable after the Restoration, and (below) a carved oak chair of about 1630.

Archbishop William Laud (1573–1645) advised and assisted Charles I in his attack on the Puritans. This policy was intended to unify the English Church and to suppress all criticism of the Crown. But the persecution only hardened the resistance of the Puritans and was a principal cause of the Civil War.

freedom of expression for his ideas than could be expected within the Church of England under King Charles I and his favourite prelate, William Laud, who became Archbishop of Canterbury in 1633.

The English Church was deeply divided. Queen Elizabeth I, when she restored Protestantism, had made a settlement which had been designed to include within the fold those who rejected the supremacy of Rome but did not otherwise wish to see much change, as well as those who subscribed to the "reformed" doctrines of Calvinism. Essentially Calvinist ideas such as redemption by Grace alone, pre-destination and the existence of a chosen *élite* of "saved" persons were widely accepted within the Church of England. But the Established Church utterly rejected the Calvinist system of organization, with lay elders and elected ministers. It had retained the time-honoured organization of the ancient Church, with Archbishops, Bishops and priests and the system of payment by tithes. Only, the sovereign had taken the place of the Pope as the supreme controller of the ecclesiastical hierarchy.

This politically ingenious compromise was repellent to some extremists, the original "Puritan" group of ministers who had been excluded from the Church before the end of Queen Elizabeth's reign. But there still existed within the Church a large number of clergy and laymen who, without wishing to sever themselves from the Church, wished to see a further Protestant reformation carried out from within, and who, in the meantime, did not always conform to the practices and rituals laid down in

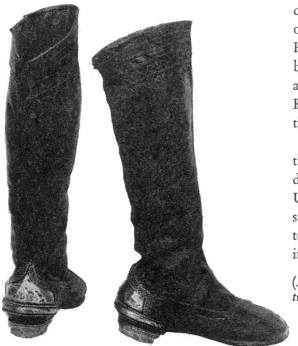

One of a pair of magnificently embroidered gloves reputed to have belonged to Charles I, and a pair of embroidered leather boots believed to have been made for him when he was a boy.

the Prayer Book. This delicate situation became explosive when King Charles I set out to strengthen the authority of the Bishops and to enforce uniformity of ritual.

While Milton was studying at Cambridge, King Charles called three Parliaments and quarrelled in succession with each of them. In 1629 he dissolved the last after a violent scene in the House of Commons, during which a group of Puritan members overpowered the Speaker and defiantly passed resolutions against the King's Church policy. After the dissolution, the King imprisoned the culprits without trial and let it be known that he would govern in future without Parliament.

Events such as these must have had a deep effect on the thoughtful young scholar at Cambridge. Gradually he abandoned all idea of entering the Church and, on leaving the University, planned to devote several years to further intensive study. The prospect he had in mind—that of preparing himself to make some important but unspecified contribution to the intellectual life of his country—must have seemed somewhat

(Above) *Charles I (1600–1649) at the age of twenty-eight—the third year of his reign.*

vague and remote to his father who had spent so much on his education. But he had great faith in him, and continued to give him unstinting help and support. The old scrivener had by this time retired from business and was living not far from London in the riverside village of Hammersmith. Here, and later at Horton in Bedfordshire, Milton spent the next five years under the paternal roof working through a prodigious programme of reading in many languages to achieve something like that wide general knowledge which he believed to be the ideal foundation of wisdom.

He was not altogether cut off from the world for he had several friends, chief among them Charles Diodati, whom he visited and with whom he carried on a lively and sometimes argumentative correspondence. He also wrote two great poems, the masque of *Comus* and the elegy we know as *Lycidas*.

The writing of *Comus* shows the young Milton in an unusually easy and elegant mood. Masques were then the fashionable form of entertainment, and a delightful fashion it was. They had been encouraged and developed at Court by Anne of Denmark, a discriminating patron of the arts, the wife of James I. Yearly she and her ladies had performed in masques, often written for them by Ben Jonson with scenery and dresses by Inigo Jones. A masque generally had a topical theme, but it was in reality little more than a vehicle for songs, dances and pleasing stage effects. Where the Court led, the nobility followed, and masques were often given at weddings or on other occasions for rejoicing.

In 1634 the amiable Earl of Bridgewater was sent to govern the borders of Wales. He had in his household as music master to his family a composer of some distinction, Henry Lawes, who was also a friend of Milton. Lawes encouraged the Earl's three children to receive their father, when he came to take up his official residence in Ludlow Castle, with a masque suitable to the happy occasion. He turned to John Milton for the words.

Their joint production, *Comus*, is outstandingly the most beautiful of the many masques written in England during this halcyon time. It tells the story of a young girl lost in a dark forest and there captured by Comus, a wild demi-god, son of Circe and Bacchus. He tempts her, in vain, to drink a magic

A suit of armour which was made for Charles II as a boy when he was Prince of Wales—the Stuart "S" is prominently displayed on the visor.

To the Some of the spull dysburgth
months is from Ester 1632 vntoll } 42 - 14 - 07
Ester 1633 for and to y pooer is

The spull prayses this yeare of
the insubysunes at torre vollaryes } 42 - 16 - 02
and by bonyfurther is

So wo ar out more then theire   00 - 01 - 05
bine collected by vs

Mo that this accompt was x vj d and
refl vx b vj d whose names are sprvbid
written att oy s daie of maie 1633 And
it apeereth vnto vs that the ovrseers
ehad xxxxxxxxx this daie and
rewarid 1 b 9 d and it doy not
apeere but vs hat yere and mony
by me carried to be collertll

Allowed

Jo: Finch

Tho: Marlynt

John Wallis

Petor Crooke
Richard Egilton
the marke of William thawart

Jo: miltone

Richard Crooke

The Milton family's short residence in Hammersmith, then a village on the banks of the Thames not far from London, is here marked by John Milton senior's signature as an auditor of the accounts of the Overseers of the Poor for that district.

Scriveners' knives, which they used for sharpening their quill pens.

potion which will put her for ever in his power, but she withstands him and is rescued at the critical moment by her two brothers. Lady Alice, who played the part of the Lady, was fifteen; her brothers and rescuers were respectively eleven and nine.

Unlike most masques, *Comus* has something serious to say. It is an allegory of the perpetual conflict of good and evil, expressed with uncompromising clarity, although set in words of exquisite lyric beauty and worked into a story perfectly suited to the young performers and the pleasant family occasion.

Three years later Milton was asked to contribute an elegy to a memorial volume planned by the friends of Edward King, a young Cambridge scholar, who had been drowned shortly after his ordination on his way to take up an appointment in Ireland. Such memorial volumes were common in Milton's time and some of them contain, among much indifferent verse, one or two contributions which have stood the test of time. Milton's *Lycidas* towers above all the rest in the slim volume sacred to the memory of Edward King. Its theme was much stronger and more personal than anything he had yet written. The premature death of one of the ablest and most attractive of his Cambridge contemporaries naturally aroused in him serious thoughts on mortality and the meaning of life. What was he doing with his own life? What if he should die before he could offer to the world the ripe fruits of all his years of preparation and win the fame for which he had toiled so long?

The principal court entertainment of the seventeenth century was the masque. Inigo Jones was a highly successful designer of both sets and costumes, of which this is an example.

> Fame is the spur that the clear spirit doth raise
> (That last infirmity of Noble mind)
> To scorn delights, and live laborious days;
> But the fair Guerdon when we hope to find,
> And think to burst out into sudden blaze,
> Comes the blind Fury with th' abhorred shears,
> And slits the thin-spun life.

Political as well as private themes run through *Lycidas*. In 1637, the year of Edward King's death, three Puritan critics of the King's government—William Prynne, Henry Burton and John Bastwick—were condemned to the pillory, to the loss of their ears and to life-long imprisonment. The savage punishment evoked widespread popular outcry. In the same year John Hampden was prosecuted for refusing to pay ship-money on the grounds that the tax had been imposed without consent of Parliament. In Scotland, also during this critical year, there began an organized revolt against the King's attempt to impose the Anglican ritual on the Scottish Church.

Inevitably therefore, the tide of political feeling runs strongly through *Lycidas*, and in lines which vibrate with passion he lamented the death of the virtuous Edward King and condemned the corrupt and neglectful clergy:

18

A drawing of London Bridge from the autograph album of a Dutch visitor to London in 1614. On the left is the tower of St. Mary Overy in Southwark, and on the right are Old St. Paul's and Gresham's Royal Exchange.

Het Haene gefecht Jn Engelandt,

Cockfighting was a popular sport of the time. This is another album drawing of what is presumed to be the Cockpit at Whitehall with James I as one of the spectators.

How well could I have spared for thee, young swain,
Enow of such as for their bellies' sake,
Creep and intrude, and climb into the fold?
Of other care they little reckoning make,
Than how to scramble at the shearers' feast,
And shove away the worthy bidden guest.
Blind mouths! that scarce themselves know how to hold
A Sheep-hook, or have learnt aught else the least
That to the faithful Herdman's art belongs!
What recks it them? What need they? They are sped:
And when they list, their lean and flashy songs
Grate on their scrannel Pipes of wretched straw,
The hungry Sheep look up, and are not fed,
But swoln with wind, and the rank mist they draw,
Rot inwardly, and foul contagion spread:
Besides what the grim Wolf with privy paw
Daily devours apace, and nothing said,
But that two-handed engine at the door,
Stands ready to smite once, and smite no more.

Milton was now twenty-nine years old. He had "scorned delights and lived laborious days" for the greater part of his adult life. Surely the time had come to "burst out into sudden blaze". But the last part—and the most pleasant—of his self-education was yet to come. He hinted at it in the final couplet of *Lycidas*:

At last he rose, and twitched his Mantle blue;
To-morrow to fresh Woods, and Pastures new.

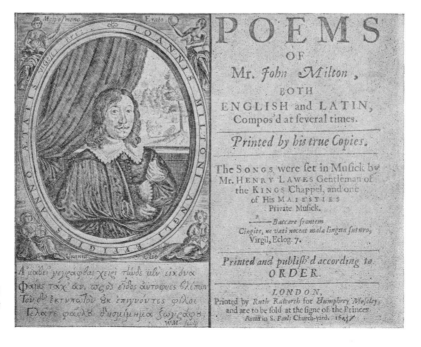

The title-page of the 1645 edition of Milton's Miscellaneous Poems.

A FEW MONTHS after writing *Lycidas* he set out to complete his education by a voyage to France and Italy. Once again his father generously and proudly financed the journey.

Italy, though politically oppressed and economically moribund, was still a place of pilgrimage and inspiration for travellers from the North and was still the centre of Europe's artistic and intellectual life. The great monuments of antiquity and the splendid achievements of the last two centuries were there for all to see. Rome, now at the height of its baroque splendour, was a magnet for painters and sculptors, and in Florence the recently founded Accademia della Crusca was a centre for philosophic speculation and inquiry. Throughout Italy numerous smaller academies and clubs of young intellectuals provided centres for interesting discussion, but the intellectual life of Italy was being gradually choked by censorship. Books or even conversations which were judged subversive to the doctrines of the Roman Church could lead to a prosecution by the Inquisition. The discreet traveller kept his opinions to himself. Milton had wisely taken advice from an experienced diplomatist, Sir Henry Wotton, before he left. The old gentleman, now Provost of Eton, had for many years been ambassador to Venice. He quoted a discreet Italian proverb to the young traveller: "Thoughts concealed and countenance open will go safely through the whole world."

So the young Puritan poet who had, in *Lycidas*, referred to the Roman Church as "the grim Wolf", concealed his disapproval and even went so far as to attend a

A replica of Galileo's telescope.

21

Galileo (1564–1642), the Italian astronomer, mathematician and physicist whom Milton visited on his journey through Europe.

reception by a Cardinal in Rome. In Florence he received a warm welcome from a group of distinguished scholars, composed verses in Latin and Italian, and made firm and lasting friendships. It must have felt to him like the first firm step on the road to international fame.

By his own account Milton appears to have talked freely in private to his Italian friends about the growing threat to their intellectual life. Later he wrote:

I have sat among their learned men and been counted happy to be born in such a place of philosophic freedom as they supposed England was, while themselves did nothing but bemoan the servile condition into which learning amongst them was brought: that this it was which had damped the glory of Italian wits; that nothing had been there written now those many years but flattery and fustian. There it was that I found and visited the famous Galileo, grown old, a prisoner of the Inquisition for thinking of astronomy otherwise than the Franciscan and Dominican licensers thought.

Milton's journey took him as far as Naples. He had planned to go on by sea to

22

Sicily and thence to Athens, but in Naples he heard of the death of his friend, Charles Diodati. The political news from England was also disturbing. Saddened and anxious, he turned homewards. He broke the journey at Venice; the great maritime republic always exerted a strong fascination over Englishmen who studied her ancient constitution and admired the skill with which she resisted the political influence of Spain and the Vatican which had spread over the rest of Italy. He passed through Geneva, the centre of Calvinist theology, and stopped in Paris where he visited Hugo Grotius, the famous Dutch pioneer of international law. Grotius too had run into trouble in his native land and had had to seek asylum in France. On all sides, therefore, Milton saw the baleful effect of religious and political division on freedom of thought, and the evidence of suppressive intervention by Church and State.

With his mind full of these things, he returned to England in the summer of 1639, fully aware that a serious crisis was impending. King Charles had by this time decided to make an end of all opposition by a display of force. The Scots had banded themselves together by the National Covenant of 1638 to resist his religious policy. His answer was to lead an army over the border. When this invasion proved a fiasco, he planned a second and more massive onslaught and called an English Parliament to vote money for it. The Commons refused to do so and his attempts to raise troops foundered on the opposition of his English subjects. Instead of a triumphant invasion of Scotland, the King found himself attacked by Scots and English alike. Defeated and bankrupt, he was compelled to call a new Parliament in November, 1640. He was powerless to resist them. They tried and executed his first minister, the Earl of Strafford. They sent the Archbishop of Canterbury, William Laud, to the Tower. They released and rewarded the Puritan critics of the royal government. The King was compelled to abolish the Prerogative Courts through which he had enforced his personal power. He was compelled to accept a bill perpetuating the existence of the present Parliament until such time as they chose to dissolve themselves. Faced by an ultimate demand to relinquish the control of the armed forces to Parliament, he refused. Fatally, he now tried, with the help of his personal guards, to re-establish his power by a military *coup*. He planned to arrest the five principal leaders of the House of Commons as they sat in session. This ill-conceived plan failed and, in the ensuing riots, he thought best to flee from London. The inevitable Civil War broke out in the summer of 1642.

Military handbooks were produced in order to show men how to handle their arms. These two drawings are from the Musket and Pike Drill respectively.

MILTON HAD taken a house in London on his return from his foreign journey. He must have witnessed the waves of excitement which swept through the City during these tense months. Gangs of seamen stormed the Archbishop's palace in Lambeth; crowds of apprentices mobbed the King's Court at Whitehall and choked the approaches to Parliament, vociferously threatening his supporters. But the mobs, sometimes spontaneous, more often organized, were only the outward manifestation of deep-rooted discontent and bitter opposition to the King. The City authorities received and sheltered the Five Members when they narrowly escaped seizure and supported the war preparations of Parliament with loans and men and arms.

Milton was in London when the King, in his first campaign, all but took the City; he was in London when the Royalist forces were checked just in time at Turnham Green. He was in London when the apprentices, formed into regiments, set out on the long march to the relief of Puritan Gloucester, close-besieged by the King's army; he was in London when they returned, and marched victorious through the streets crowned with green leaves. He was in London when a Royalist *coup* failed and the conspirators were executed, hanged before their own doors. He would have known of the trial and execution of Roman Catholic priests; and rejoiced at the beheading on Tower Hill of Archbishop Laud, once the scourge of the Puritans, but now a poor, tottering old man.

It was a long war. London suffered from shortage of fuel, food and trade. Yet many citizens were sustained and inspired by the fervent belief that liberty and spiritual regeneration would follow the victory of Parliament. In Milton's words, they hoped for "such a deliverance as shall never be forgotten by any revolution of time that this world hath to finish".

A pair of heavy jack-boots made of stout black leather.

A buff coat, probably designed for an officer, and a buff coat and bandolier. These coats were made of cow hide and could stop a sword slash.

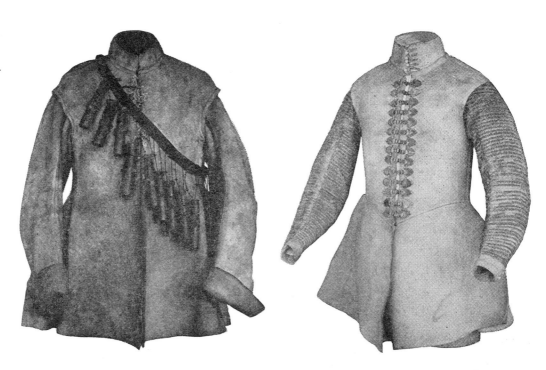

Milton had been caught up from the beginning in the blaze of pamphlet warfare which characterized the Civil War. On the collapse of King Charles's government fear of prosecution was lifted and immediately any man (and some women) with ideas began to publish them abroad. Religious controversy was the most usual subject, with political argument next; but there were also pamphlets on everything, from the improvement of agriculture to the foundation of new universities.

Now was the moment when Milton held it a duty to help his country in its hour of destiny by setting forth his own considered ideas for open discussion. And yet he hated the vulgar din of popular debate and yearned to pursue his studies uninterrupted and to compose the great epic poem in English which he envisaged as his life's work. "With what small willingness," he wrote, "I endure to . . . leave a calm and pleasing solitariness fed with cheerful thoughts to embark in a troubled sea of noises and harsh disputes." At first he joined in the general argument about the nature of the reform that the national church should undergo. A little later he composed his tractate *Of Education*, a plea for more modern and imaginative methods in schools and universities. The subject was frequently canvassed at the time among men of learning, and Milton may even have met the famous Czech educationist, John Comenius, who visited England on the eve of the Civil War in response to an invitation from a group of English admirers. He was certainly influenced by another foreigner, Samuel Hartlib, a native of the Baltic states who had made his home in England, was a prosperous merchant in London, and used his means and his leisure for many years for the propagation of every kind of useful knowledge. Milton's interest in education in the meantime found practical expression in teaching the two sons of his sister Anne, who were exposed to his imaginative if somewhat strenuous ideas of a training in the classics.

A siege armour. Metal supports between the helmet and shoulder plates relieved the wearer's neck of much of the helmet's weight and also distributed the force of any blow on the head by missiles being hurled from above by the defenders of the garrison.

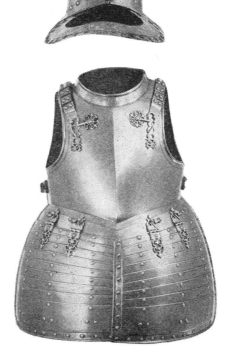

A sixteenth-century cuirassier's armour (far left) adapted for use by one of the Earl of Pembroke's retainers. Only two troops of cuirassiers were in use during the Civil War, both on the Parliamentary side, and these only for a short time, as such elaborate sets of armour were difficult to repair when damaged. Most officers and mounted troopers wore steel helmets, breast- and back-plates over buff coats and carried a brace of pistols and a broadsword.

A pikeman's armour, consisting of a broad-brimmed helmet, breast- and back-plates and square tasses on the thighs.

Though the affairs of the nation absorbed and inspired him, his own private affairs were not in such a hopeful state. A few months before the outbreak of the Civil War he had married a young wife. He was thirty-four; his bride was seventeen. She was the daughter of a feckless country squire named Powell, who had borrowed money from Milton's father. Mary Powell was beautiful and—as he thought—modest and docile. The wooing scarcely lasted a month, and it was not until the marriage knot was irrevocably tied that Milton realized, to his chagrin and dismay, that she was totally unequipped to profit by his intellectual conversation or to share any of his serious interests. After a few weeks she withdrew to her family in Oxfordshire, ostensibly for a short visit. They were Royalists, and when the war broke out she refused altogether to return to him in London.

Humiliated and raging Milton produced his pamphlet on the reform of the Divorce Laws. *The Doctrine and Discipline of Divorce* is not an attractive piece of work; it is too evidently inspired by his own disappointment and sense of personal grievance. Yet it drew attention to a real social evil. The conventions of the time made it nearly impossible for young men and women of the educated classes to form any judgement of each other before marriage. Divorce was virtually unknown except to the very rich and powerful, and hundreds of ill-assorted couples were left to ruin each other's lives.

By the time the divorce pamphlet was published in 1643, Parliament was thoroughly alarmed at the number of dangerous and unconventional ideas appearing in print. In the House of Commons some members advocated the imposition of censorship. This inspired Milton to write and publish in the following year, 1644, the most famous of all his pamphlets, the great appeal for freedom of the press which he called *Areopagitica* after the Areopagus, the democratic assembly of Athens. This most quoted of all his works is an eloquent appeal to Parliament, to the Lords and Commons of England, to accept the consequences of their own brave actions in challenging the government of the King. It was their action, in opposing the King and standing up for the liberty of the subject, which had unleashed the free writing and the free speaking which now abounded in England. Would they now destroy that very liberty which they had

No new styles in dress evolved in Commonwealth times; there were merely levels between plainness of attire and frivolity. Dark materials in simple styles, with plain collars and cuffs, worn with tall black hats were usually regarded as being a sign of extreme Puritan views, and were by no means standard dress for supporters of Cromwell's régime.

created? "Who kills a man kills a reasonable creature, God's image; but he who destroys a good book kills reason itself . . ."

This noble plea embodied not only Milton's faith in the power of Truth ("Let her and Falsehood grapple; whoever knew Truth put to the worse in a free and open encounter?"), but also his faith in England, the new England that he believed would arise

The disposition of the armies of Charles I and General Fairfax at the Battle of Naseby, fought on June 14, 1645. The result was a defeat for the King by the New Model Army, whose right wing was commanded by Cromwell.

(Far right) *The frontispiece of Milton's* Areopagitica *published in 1644.*

from the fires of Civil War. "Methinks I see in my mind a noble and puissant nation rousing herself like a strong man after sleep and shaking her invincible locks. Methinks I see her as an eagle mewing her mighty youth, and kindling her undazzled eyes at the full midday beam."

Political disillusion was to follow when the war came to an end, but also a return

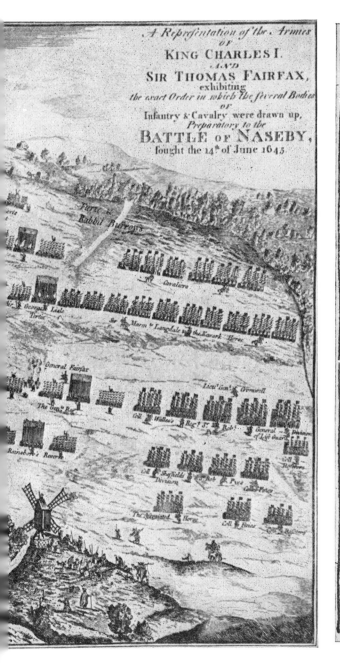

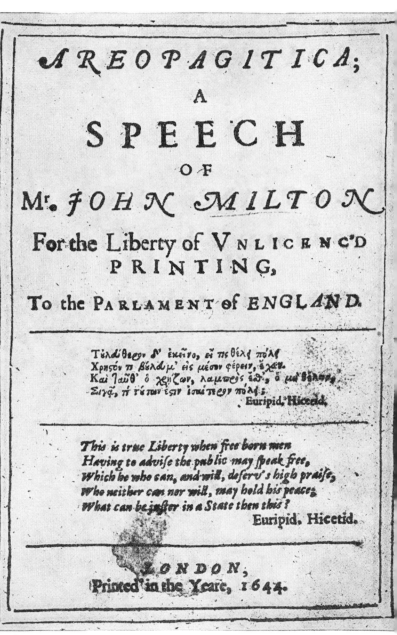

A child's quilted gown.

*An attractive early seventeenth-century cos-
tume. The bodice and skirt are of white linen
with black silk embroidery.*

of personal happiness. After the defeat of the King in 1646 the Powell family, like many other Royalists, were in dire poverty. Friends of Milton arranged a meeting between the injured husband and his now penitent wife. She was still only a little over twenty and he was touched by her beauty and her tears. As his nephew was later to describe it, he agreed to an "Act of Oblivion" as to the past and entered into a firm "League of Peace" for the future. Not only did he take her back, but he offered the hospitality of his house to her entire (and not very grateful) family. Thenceforward their marrage seems to have been reasonably happy. She bore him two daughters, and a son who died in infancy. In 1652 she died, like so many women at that time, in giving birth to a third daughter. He commemorated her with touching and tender feeling in the sonnet beginning "Methought I saw my late espoused saint . . ."

He was to marry again—twice. Catherine Woodhouse, his second wife, died after only two years of marriage, and is little more than a shadow in his biography. His third wife, Elizabeth Minshall—he called her "Betty"—was an excellent cook who pampered him; and by that time he had ceased to expect intellectual companionship from the womenfolk of his household.

A rather cheerless-looking Puritan doll, made of wood.

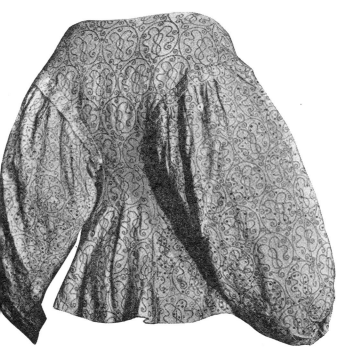

An embroidered linen cap of the sort that men wore indoors, and (below) a pair of green silk embroidered shoes in the extravagant fashion of Charles II's court.

Dress bodices belonging (above) to the early seventeenth-century and (left) to the sixteen-sixties. These bodices were worn with full, softly-gathered skirts, and at the time of the Restoration it became fashionable to wear wide lace collars over the low necklines.

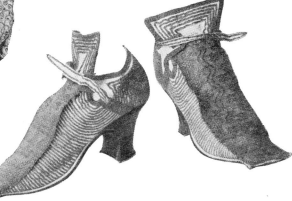

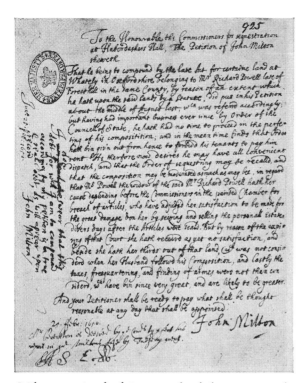

Milton was involved in many legal disputes over the Oxfordshire estate of his first wife's father, Richard Powell, which had been mortgaged many times over. He was going blind at the time this particular petition was submitted to Haberdashers' Hall in 1650, so only the signature and the marginal note are in Milton's own handwriting.

THE YEARS immediately following the King's defeat were politically disheartening to a man of Miltons' strong but unworldly idealism. He watched with anger the unworthy attempts of the Presbyterian party in Parliament to curb the religious liberty for which, in his opinion, the war had been fought, and to disband without payment the Army which had won it. But the King's intrigues provoked a second Civil War and this precipitated a crisis in which the Army, victorious for a second time, forcibly purged the House of Commons, took control of the nation's affairs and, under the leadership of Oliver Cromwell, brought the King to trial.

Milton saw this event as a notable example of the justice of God on a tyrant who had betrayed his people, and he believed that his death would make way for a just government founded on popular consent. He was in the phraseology of his own time a "Commonwealthman". His ideas were based partly on the Bible, in which wicked Kings were often the objects of divine vengeance, and partly on his classical studies which had given to him, as to many of his contemporaries, a somewhat exaggerated view of the virtues of the Roman Republic.

While the King's trial absorbed the attention of all England in that cold January of 1649, Milton thought the matter out for himself among his books. A few days after the execution of King Charles he published a political pamphlet of great lucidity and power called *The Tenure of Kings and Magistrates*. Kings, he argued, hold their power by virtue of a tacit contract with the people. They are the stewards of the commonwealth. If they fail in their stewardship—and Charles I had palpably failed—they could be called to account by the people. This theory of monarchical government was not new. It had been worked out during the previous century to justify both the religious wars in France and the revolt of the Dutch against Philip II of Spain. Many pamphlets and sermons against the King during these critical days made use of the same arguments. They were heard also from John Bradshaw, the President of the Court which tried the King and from John Cook who prosecuted him. But they are nowhere set forth with more clarity and strength than in Milton's *Tenure*.

Such a statement of the case against Charles was needed, for he had behaved during his trial and on the scaffold with a courage and dignity that impressed even his enemies and gave him, in the eyes of his loyal friends, heroic and even saintly stature. Immediately after his death a Royalist printer issued a slim volume of thoughts and prayers said to have been composed by the King in his captivity. It was called *Eikon Basilike*: the King's Image. The little book had an instant and phenomenal success. In spite of government efforts to stifle it, it was re-printed thirty-five times before the end of the year. The King appears in it as a Christian martyr devoutly enduring the persecution of wicked men.

To counteract its effect the government resolved to issue an answer and turned to Milton to compose it. It was his first official connection with the newly formed Commonwealth of England, and though he—rightly in this case—doubted his power to nullify the effect of *Eikon Basilike*, he was glad to serve the supposedly free republican government in which he believed. His book, *Eikonoklastes*—The Image Breaker, cannot be accounted one of his most successful. It has the personally vindictive tone which characterized much contemporary pamphleteering and which today alienates rather than attracts.

A more serious task soon followed. The Royalists in exile commissioned one of the most famous scholars in Europe to write a Latin defence of the martyred King and to denounce the upstart government formed by his murderers. The author, Claude de Saumaise, internationally known by his latinized name as Salmasius, was a conceited pedant with an immense and largely unjustified reputation. It was important, none the less, that an effective answer be made to his attack, and once again the government turned to Milton as perhaps the only Englishman who commanded a Latin style that would be more than a match for the famous Salmasius. Milton's answer *Pro Populo Anglicano Defensio—In Defence of the English People* contains a virulent personal attack on

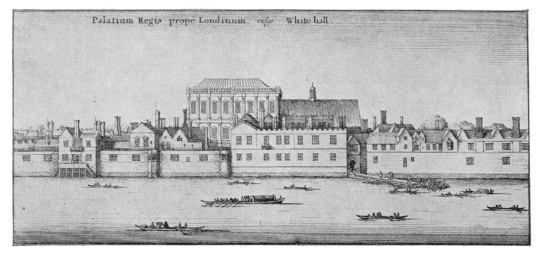

The new Banqueting Hall, built by Inigo Jones in 1619–1622, towers over the more humble buildings of the old Palace of Whitehall by the River Thames. John Evelyn, the diarist, recorded in April, 1647, that "the rebel army" was "quartering at Whitehall". In 1698 Whitehall Palace was burned to the ground, though the Banqueting Hall still survives.

33

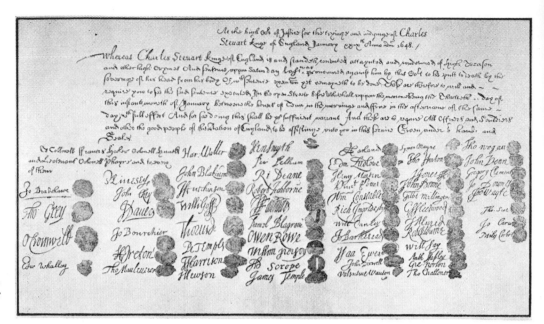

Charles I's death warrant, with Cromwell's signature in the left-hand column.

Salmasius—an attack which did much to puncture his inflated reputation. More effective was his well-argued point by point refutation of the monarchist arguments put forward by Salmasius. There was nothing "defensive", in the modern sense, about Milton's defence of the English Republic and the King's execution. Indeed, he gloried in the act and concluded his book with a trumpet call to his countrymen to go on to yet greater things:

> After so glorious a deed, you ought to think, you ought to do nothing that is mean and petty, nothing but what is great and sublime. To attain such praise there is only one way: as you have subdued your enemies in the field, so you shall prove that unarmed and surrounded by peace you of all mankind have the highest courage to subdue what conquers other nations—faction, avarice, the temptations of wealth and the corruptions that wait upon prosperity.

During the composition of the *Defensio*, Milton had finally gone blind. His sight had troubled him seriously for some time before he began on it, and he himself believed that his work on it had brought on total blindness. It was a sacrifice he gladly made in the service of his country. Others, he wrote with proud resignation, had given their lives for the English Commonwealth; he had made a lesser sacrifice—his sight. But it was for him a very dreadful sacrifice none the less, for he had deeply loved the beauty of the world—flowers, sunlight, green fields, the open skies, the faces of those he loved. Modern research now suggests that his blindness was not caused or even hastened in

34

any way by his studies, but he believed that it was so, and his self-sacrifice in continuing his work must still be admired.

He had been appointed to other posts under the new government. Only a few weeks after the King's death, in March, 1649, he became Latin Secretary, responsible for overseeing and in great measure composing all government correspondence with foreign powers. Royalists abroad decried the new masters of England as low-born illiterate scoundrels. So it was important to make a good showing in diplomacy by employing one of the most erudite and graceful Latinists in Europe.

Two years later in 1651 he was appointed Chief Censor, with the special task of supervising the government-inspired newspaper *Mercurius Politicus*. How could John Milton, author of *Areopagitica*, reconcile his belief in freedom of opinion with his present task of government censor? In effect Milton was prepared to license any serious book that did not endanger the government in which he believed and which was open to attack on so many sides. The Royalists naturally did not cease from abusing it. The Presbyterians, who had wanted to reform rather than destroy the monarchy and to impose a single national Church of their own design, were bitterly hostile, and counted among their number some of the best pamphleteers in the country. Then there was the highly vocal group called the Levellers, whose spokesman was the vigorous and fanatical John Lilburne. They hated the new government because it had not gone far enough; they wanted far-reaching reforms of the Parliamentary system and the law in the interests of artisans, yeomen, craftsmen—all the respectable hard-working small men who had never yet had a say in the nation's affairs. There were splinter groups like the Diggers, led by Gerard Winstanley, who advocated (and tried to practise) the common ownership of land. All of these were prolific in pamphlets, many of them of a highly inflammatory kind.

Furthermore, London teemed with newspapers. The newspaper was a Dutch invention of the 1620s. The idea had spread rapidly to France, where the astute Cardinal Richelieu had immediately taken them in hand—permitting only one excellent but government-controlled newspaper. King Charles I, far less perceptive, had forbidden the publication of newspapers in England. With the collapse of his government, newspapers sprang up like weeds. They were little pamphlets of eight or sixteen pages, each appearing once a week and

A contemporary engraving of Charles I's execution outside the Banqueting Hall at Whitehall.

35

containing a brief day-to-day summary of current events with a few lines of commentary and sometimes an opening paragraph of general reflections, the ancestor of the modern "leader". As each editor (or printer) tried to secure a different publication day, the news-eager Londoner could buy at least one newly printed paper every day of the week. Some of them lasted only for a few numbers; others went on for a number of years. The Levellers, forerunners in this as in so many other ways, had their own mouthpiece, a well-run news sheet called *The Moderate*.

Throughout the war and in the succeeding years Parliament, from time to time, suppressed a paper or arrested an editor who had overstepped the mark. The Commonwealth government, imitating Richelieu, decided to take one paper under its patronage as an instrument of propaganda and policy. This was *Mercurius Politicus*, edited by a brilliant, witty, fickle journalist named Marchamont Nedham, who had run a Parliamentary paper during the Civil War, then allowed himself to be bought by the King and had for some months issued a clandestine Royalist paper before reverting, possibly under the personal influence of Milton, to his more natural bent. It was an odd partnership this, between the grave blind poet with his high faith in the destiny of the Commonwealth and the brisk time-serving journalist. But Nedham had a good mind and a clear command of language. Milton evidently liked him, and for twelve months the partnership worked successfully. At the end of that time Milton was dismissed from his post as censor. He had licensed the publication in England of the so-called *Racovian Catechism*—a notorious heretical work which denied the doctrine of the Trinity. Summoned before the Council of State, he pointed out that he had acted according to his own principles as expressed in *Areopagitica*. If these principles were unacceptable to the government he could no longer continue as Censor. He thus ceased to control the press, but he retained his important post as Latin Secretary.

New Palace Yard in the seventeenth century. On the right is the Clock Tower, and on the left is the great Westminster Hall, the scene of the trial of Charles I. The remaining buildings were undistinguished and included ale-houses and coffee shops.

36

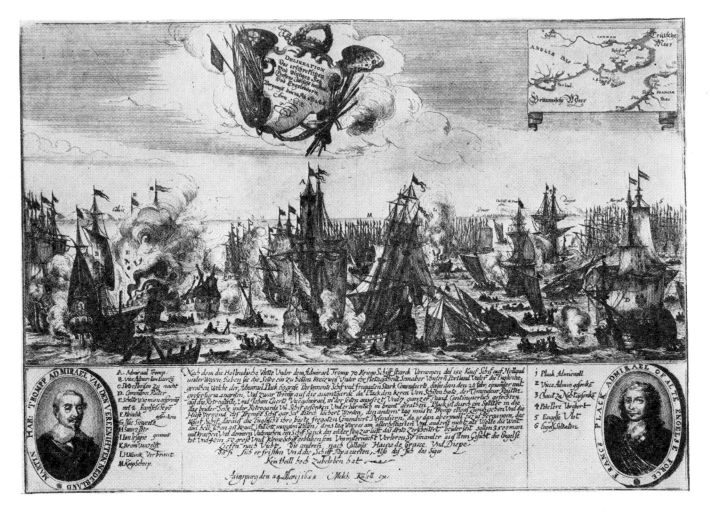

FOR JOHN MILTON, as for some other idealists, the years immediately following the King's death were bright with hope for the establishment of a just and righteous government, called by some the Rule of the Saints. Remarkable events encouraged this belief. Ireland and Scotland, which had both declared for King Charles II, were speedily subdued by Cromwell. The Dutch, who thought that the English were exhausted by Civil War, attacked them by sea; they were totally and dismayingly defeated by the great new ships which Parliament had built and the superb seamanship of the Puritan commanders, Robert Blake, Richard Deane, Edward Popham and others. Fifty years from the death of Queen Elizabeth I, after a long eclipse, England became almost overnight mistress of the seas.

But at home the Commonwealth government was in a state of total confusion. Parliament, the remnant of the assembly which had first met in 1640, failed to evolve a

A contemporary print of the Battle of Portland, which took place in March, 1653. This was an important encounter in the First Dutch War, as Robert Blake defeated Admiral Tromp's fleet whose mission had been to escort a fleet of homebound Dutch merchantmen back through the English Channel. Without command of the Channel Dutch trade was severely hampered. Here the English fleet is seen advancing from the right and the ships of the two admirals are exchanging broadsides in the foreground.

(Left) *Oliver Cromwell (1599–1658)—the Lord Protector.*

Robert Blake (1599–1657) is best known as the admiral who made the Cromwellian navy all-powerful at sea in a series of remarkable victories. Yet he made his reputation as a soldier in the Parliamentary army. By land and sea he was a man of outstanding skill and courage, and much beloved by his men.

new constitution for the state or to make way for a new Parliament that would do so. It had long ceased to be in any way representative of the nation. Cromwell, victorious in Ireland and Scotland, took the law into his own hands and forcibly dissolved it in March 1653. A new Parliament met, popularly called Barebone's Parliament in mockery of a prominent member, Praisegod Barebone, whose name seemed to typify extreme Puritan piety. This Parliament intended to implement the Rule of the Saints, but leaned too far towards radical change to satisfy the substantial citizens of London whose loans financed the government. This short-lived, idealistic assembly resigned its authority into the hands of the only man who had the power, the reputation and the courage to accept responsibility—Oliver Cromwell.

Cromwell, who took the title of Lord Protector, made an honest attempt to rule as he believed England should be ruled—by consent of Parliament. But there were too many unreconciled groups in the country. No truly representative Parliament could be called, and those which he did call proved as recalcitrant and unmanageable as their predecessors under Charles I. He was driven to base his government, in the last resort, on the power of his Army. Yet he strove to govern within the framework of English legal tradition as he understood it. His government, even at its worst, was not a dictator-

38

ship in the modern sense and was far less ruthless than the government of Henry VIII, or even, in some respects, than that of Queen Elizabeth I.

The popular picture of the Cromwellian epoch as a period of joyless austerity is greatly exaggerated. Theatrical companies still performed in private houses and chamber music concerts were introduced at the Cromwellian Court as a seemly and decorous way of entertaining distinguished guests. Something in the nature of a masque was even performed at the marriage of Cromwell's youngest daughter. In 1656 the Protector granted a licence to William Davenant to re-open the theatre in Drury Lane for dramatic performances with music—the earliest opera in England.

It was in Cromwell's time that the first coffee house in London opened its doors. The fashion for social meetings over a cup of the dark liquid caught on and soon the intelligent society of the capital began to use the coffee houses as informal clubs for the discussion of ideas and current events.

Other societies and clubs, meeting in private houses in London or elsewhere, had grown up since the closing years of the Civil War—clubs where the latest inventions and explorations in the natural sciences were

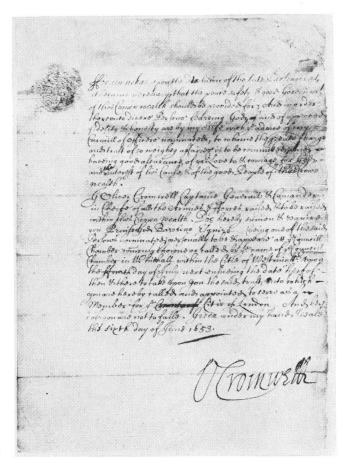

Cromwell's summons to Praisegod Barebone to appear at the Council Chamber in Whitehall as member for the City of London on July 4, 1653—the so-called "Barebone's Parliament".

Cromwell dissolving the Rump Parliament in 1653 with the words, "Begone you rogues. You have sat long enough."

The sign of the "Dish of Coffee Boy", a coffee house in seventeenth-century Brick Lane, Spitalfields. Coffee houses gradually became gathering places for all classes of people, where they drank coffee, smoked and read the latest news. Poorer people would often join together to buy a newspaper.

(Below) A token from the famous Turk's Head Coffee House. Tokens were produced by local tradesmen in order to be able to give small change to customers, there being a shortage of coins for low denominations at this time, and were usually worth a farthing or a halfpenny.

discussed and demonstrated. The most famous of these, which met in Oxford, counted among its members Robert Boyle and Christopher Wren; it was to form the nucleus of the famous Royal Society, officially founded after the Restoration, and flourishing to this day.

Whatever the virtues of his regime, Cromwell himself was hated by the Royalists as a King-murderer and usurper. He was hated almost as bitterly by many of his old friends and colleagues, the convinced Commonwealthmen, who felt that he had betrayed their conception of an ideal republic.

Milton himself had been a fervent Commonwealthman, but he had been disillusioned by the confusion and corruption of the civil government in the years following the King's death, and he welcomed Cromwell as God's chosen instrument for the preservation of the people. In some respects Cromwell did indeed seem to be a man chosen, like Joshua of old, to do great things for the nation. He carried the Dutch war to a successful conclusion and then re-knit the ancient brotherly alliance between the two great maritime peoples. He stood forth dramatically as the champion of oppressed co-religionists abroad when he took up the cause of the Vaudois, a small group of Protestants long settled in the Italian Alps, against whom the Duke of Savoy had launched a campaign of extermination. It was Milton who drafted the Protector's formidable denunciation of the Duke, and the letters which went out to France, Sweden, Switzerland, Denmark and Holland demanding an international intervention. Milton's heart was in these letters, for the poet in him was inspired at the same time to the sonnet which vibrates with indignant sympathy:

Avenge O Lord thy slaughtered Saints, whose bones
Lie scattered on the Alpine mountains cold . . .

Since his blindness he had of course had assistance in performing his task as Latin Secretary. The Secretary's work was in any case far greater than it had been for many years past owing to the active foreign policy of Cromwell. His principal helpers were the inventive and lively-minded Samuel Hartlib (an old friend), the learned poet Andrew Marvell and, towards the end, a young scholar called John Dryden. Can any government at any time have employed quite so striking a team to draft its diplomatic messages?

With the death of Cromwell on September 3, 1658, the fabric of government crumbled. The Army forced the resignation of his unwarlike son Richard who had been appointed to succeed him as Protector. After Richard's fall came eighteen months of dizzy uncertainty while the old Commonwealthmen wrestled for power with the ambitious army officers who strove to set up a new military protectorate. Meanwhile educated men speculated freely in the coffee houses. At one of them, the Turk's Head, a club named the Rota gave itself up wholly to discussing theories of government and an ideal constitution to be imposed upon England. The leading figure was James Harrington, but the crude logic of political events caught up all too soon with him and his speculative circle. General George Monk, who had been for the last five years governor of Scotland, ultimately marched on London and peacefully saved the situation by declaring for the restoration of the legitimate sovereign. After twelve years of exile Charles II rode into London amid scenes of extravagant rejoicing. Swarthy, sardonic, smiling and disillusioned, he was to be, personally, the most popular King England ever had.

The majority welcomed the return to traditional government. But a considerable minority faced the future with misgiving or despair and cursed the fickle folly of a nation which had fought for its liberty only to return willingly to its chains. Milton, as he followed with increasing anguish the collapse of the cause he had served, appealed to his countrymen in a pamphlet called *The Ready and Easy Way to Establish a Free Commonwealth*. This frantic last minute appeal against the monarchy had no effect. Its publication, within a few weeks of the Restoration, together with Milton's earlier writings against King Charles I, seemed to his friends to mark him out for vengeance from the new King. They persuaded him to go into hiding.

The restored King had promised pardon to all those who were not excepted by name on the request of Parliament. The case of John Milton came up in June 1660 and there were many in the vengefully Royalist

Andrew Marvell (1621–1678). His intelligence and integrity were recognised by Milton, who recommended him as his assistant in the post of Latin Secretary to the Commonwealth Government.

The reverse of the Dunbar Medal struck in 1650 to commemorate Cromwell's defeat of the Covenanters' army at Dunbar. The Scots had declared Charles II to be King and had refused to recognise the English republic.

The two seven-pound woolweights (left) belong to the Charles I and Commonwealth periods respectively, and bear the appropriate coats of arms. Wool was the staple manufacture of England at this time, both for the home market and for export, and was carefully weighed in bales of seven pounds weight, or multiples of seven pounds.

House of Commons who would have exempted him from pardon. But his old friend and one time assistant, Andrew Marvell, now Member of Parliament for Hull, spoke for him and was joined in his plea by the Royalist poet William Davenant. Even Milton's enemies were impressed by the argument that God had already punished him by blindness: it would be blasphemy for men to add anything to the divine judgement. So John Milton was included under the benefits of the Act of Indemnity and crept cautiously out of hiding.

> Now blind, dishearten'd, sham'd, dishonour'd, quell'd,
> To what can I be useful, wherein serve
> My Nation . . .?

The tragic words which he put into the mouth of blind Samson may well, at this time, have expressed his own feelings. It was for him and for those who felt as he did an agonizing year. He would have heard of the exhumation and dishonouring of Cromwell's body, and of all the bodies of those who had faithfully served the Commonwealth, the great seaman Robert Blake among them. He would have known of the ghastly deaths of men who had been his colleagues, his close friends—some by the horrible method of hanging and quartering, others (among them his old friend Harry Vane) by the more merciful method of the axe. The great adventure towards civil freedom and righteous government had ended in contempt and shame.

Mid-seventeenth-century male dress had begun to evolve from the reign of James I, when hats became low-crowned and wide-brimmed, ruffs were replaced by wide collars, breeches became longer and tighter and shoes were replaced by long boots with wide or turned-down tops.

Charles II (1630–1685) who reigned from 1660 to 1685. His restoration to the throne could have meant death for Milton.

BUT HE still had the luminous inner world of his inspiration. He still had his life-long ambition to create a great epic poem in the great English language. The muse had not forsaken him:

> Standing on Earth, not rapt above the Pole;
> More safe I sing, with mortal voice unchang'd
> To hoarse or mute, though fall'n on evil days,
> On evil days though fall'n, and evil tongues;
> In darkness, and with dangers compassed round,
> And solitude; yet not alone, while thou
> Visit'st my slumbers nightly, or when Morn
> Purples the East: still govern thou my song,
> Urania, and fit audience find, though few.

In his youth he had planned to write a British epic, about King Arthur. But he had long since abandoned his youthful dream and decided that the great English epic must treat of the greatest of all epic situations, the creation of the world and the Fall of Man.

Meanwhile he lived in reduced, though not uncomfortable circumstances in London with his third wife (whom he married in 1663) and his rather unsympathetic daughters. He was unlucky in that all of them took after their mother's family and had no serious interests. He was more fortunate in the number and loyalty of his friends who often helped him by reading aloud and taking down his works at dictation—a task that his daughters performed with a poor grace.

In 1665 occurred the Great Plague of London. Bubonic Plague had been endemic in Western Europe since the fourteenth century. Serious outbreaks occurred at irregular intervals. During Milton's life there had been a number of bad years—1625, 1636, 1646 . . . But the outbreak of 1665 was the worst visitation experienced for centuries. At the peak moment the number of deaths in London overtopped two thousand a week, and the total number of dead was reckoned at about sixty thousand. The horrible disease is carried by rats and communicated to human beings by fleas. People who lived in houses that were not infested by rats, and whose own bodies were not infested by fleas were safe from it. But this they did not know in Milton's time. They had other ideas about infection. They burnt aromatic fires at street corners to dispel the noxious air and they shut up the sick and sealed off their houses, thus condemning the healthy to perish with them. They snuffed at pomanders as they walked

Charles II was responsible for introducing this style of dress in 1666. The coat was long with wide cuffs, and a long "waistcoat" was worn underneath, fastened with a row of buttons like the coat. Neither coat nor waistcoat had a collar, and a lace cravat was worn round the neck. Breeches were tight-fitting and long, and natural-coloured wigs were worn.

through the streets and they believed in the high disinfectant virtue of vinegar. One brave doctor, who never left his post through the whole outbreak, said afterwards that he had preserved his own health entirely through the excellent habit of taking a glass of sherry every night and every morning.

Those who could left London. Milton was persuaded to do so. He spent the summer and autumn with his family at a small house in Chalfont St. Giles about twenty miles away from London. It was here in all probability that he put the last touches to *Paradise Lost*. Of all his earthly dwelling places, this unassuming rural retreat has alone survived to become a place of pilgrimage for his admirers from two hemispheres.

He was back in London when the plague abated in the winter, and was in his house

A trade card of John Keeling who was manufacturing early fire engines in Blackfriars in 1678.

These Engins, (which are ⟨⟩ the best) to quinch grea

in September 1666 when the Great Fire of London reduced two-thirds of the city to ruins. His own house, just outside the City walls, was safe; but his childhood home in Bread Street, his old school, and the entire region round Saint Paul's was a blackened waste, and the gothic Cathedral itself a gaunt and dangerous ruin.

In the following year he published *Paradise Lost*. The publisher, Samuel Simmons of Aldersgate Street, gave him a down payment of £5 and undertook to pay a further £5 when a first edition of thirteen hundred copies was exhausted. For second and third editions—if these were thought necessary—he was to have £5 a-piece. The agreement hardly sounds generous even if we multiply the sum by about twenty to get its equivalent value in modern terms. Yet it was by no means a bad contract by the standards of

A broadsheet published in 1665, the year of the Great Plague, cataloguing the numbers who had died of the disease during outbreaks dating from 1592 (the outbreak of 1665 being the seventh).

A plague bell. These bells were rung before the carts which collected the corpses for burial, along with the cry of "bring out your dead".

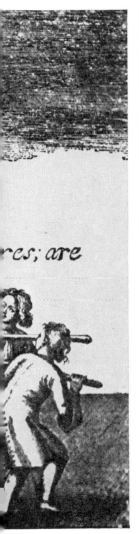

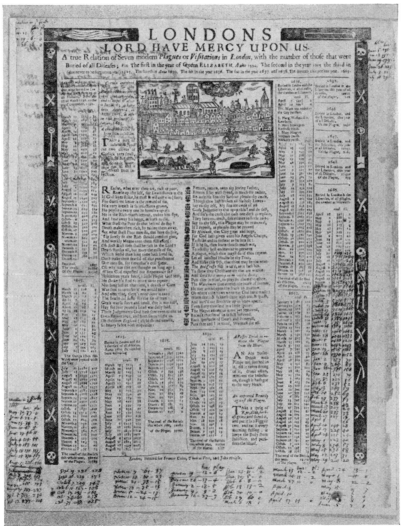

As the Fire of London had destroyed all wooden street and inn signs, they were subsequently made of stone as a precautionary measure. The inn sign, dated 1667, belonged to the Three Kings Tavern, and the street sign, dated 1670, is from Gardener's Lane, Upper Thames Street.

the time. Thirteen hundred copies was a large edition. The average printing of a pamphlet was about five hundred, and few newspapers went over a thousand. Milton was not writing to support himself, nor was he writing for a large public. He had said himself a "fit audience, though few".

This audience he found. Some voices were raised against *Paradise Lost* because it was written in blank verse at a moment when the rhymed couplet was in fashion. Milton defended himself in the preface to the second edition; he had used "English heroic verse without rhyme, as that of Homer in Greek and of Virgil in Latin, rhyme being no necessary adjunct or true ornament of a poem . . . but an invention of a barbarous age to set off wretched matter and lame meter". His poem was admired by the discriminating. John Dryden, himself the greatest master of the rhymed couplet, is said to have exclaimed, "This man cuts us all out, and the ancients too". Sir John Denham, a fashionable minor poet and another skilful master of the couplet, called *Paradise Lost* "the noblest poem that ever was wrote in any language or in any age".

The thirteen hundred copies were sold within two years. A second edition followed in 1674. Meanwhile Milton re-published his early poems, and brought out two further majestic poems of his maturity—publications which show beyond doubt that, in spite of his politics and his poverty, he was recognized and appreciated by all lovers of literature, even in the frivolous world of Charles II. *Paradise Regained* has not the scope and splendour of *Paradise Lost*, but it is a noble work on a smaller scale. *Samson Agonistes*, with its deeply felt description of blindness and defeat and the triumphant calm of its closing lines, is the nearest thing in English to the austere intensity of early Greek drama, on which it was based. It must also represent Milton's own inward and successful struggle towards serene acceptance of God's will.

46

AROUND THE blind poet hummed the busy London of Charles II. The great city had made a remarkable and rapid recovery from the Fire and was now on its way to becoming the mart of the world. Brick houses and broader streets replaced the wooden houses and narrow alleys of Milton's youth. The graceful baroque churches of Christopher Wren, with their delicate spires and towers, soared up in place of the gothic ruins. Dryden, in graceful complimentary couplets, sang the praise of the re-born city.

At Drury Lane the fashionable world attended the bawdy comedies, pretty pastorals and mannered tragedies of the Restoration stage. A permissive, tolerant, disillusioned Court set an example of elegant immorality that was copied by the aristocratic world, and shocked, while it fascinated, the more respectable part of the population. Samuel Pepys, in his Diary, recorded in lively detail the busy life of London and the gay life of the Court.

In more serious moments the King encouraged the new scientific outlook and patronized the Royal Society. The *virtuosi* as they were called—men of widely varied knowledge and interests, like John Evelyn—were the leaders of intellectual life. The mood was one of inquiry, experiment and invention. Robert Boyle and the young Isaac Newton were on the verge of great discoveries. In another sphere Sir William Petty launched something which he called "political arithmetic"; it was the beginning of the science of statistics.

It was a dark time for the Puritans who would not conform to the established Church. Presbyterians, Baptists, Quakers were oppressed, persecuted, often imprisoned. The now dominant Cavaliers ascribed all the troubles of the last half century to their influence, and a savage code of laws was enacted to control and suppress them. When Milton published *Paradise Lost*, a Baptist preacher named John Bunyan in Bedford gaol

Sir Christopher Wren (1632–1723) was responsible for the design of fifty City churches re-built after the Fire of London. The Church of St. Mary-le-Bow, Cheapside (below), shows the typical features of his designs—a simple cubic shape which harmonised with an elaborate spire.

A pastel of the sightless Milton as he looked a few years before his death. This portrait, from which many drawings and engravings are derived, is traditionally attributed to William Faithorne.

The frontispiece of Paradise Lost *published in 1667.*

Paradiſe loſt.
A
POEM
Written in
TEN BOOKS
By *JOHN MILTON.*

Licenſed and Entred according to Order.

LONDON
Printed, and are to be ſold by *Peter Parker* under *Creed* Church neer *Aldgate*; And by *Robert Boulter* at the Turks Head in *Biſhopſgate-ſtreet*; And *Matthias Walker*, under St. *Dunſtins* Church in *Fleet-ſtreet*, 1667.

was writing a prose epic of a different kind, *The Pilgrim's Progress.* The profound scholar and the unlettered preacher—one in the noblest of poetry, and the other in the simplest of prose—illuminated man's long stumbling struggle towards a lost perfection.

Milton was not unhappy in his last years. He lived peacefully, was visited by many friends, and was well cared for by his frugal wife. His enemy was the gout, yet he could be cheerful; even—as his maidservant later reported—merry in spite of it. Sometimes, remembering his youth, he would sing. "He would sit in a grey coarse cloth coat at the door of his house near Bunhill Fields within Moorgate, in warm sunny weather to enjoy the fresh air and so . . . receive the visits of people of distinguished parts, as well as quality."

He no longer attended Church, and the omission does not seem to have brought him into any trouble with the parish authorities. He thought much and deeply of the eternal mysteries, but the long treatise in which he finally summed up his views—*De Doctrina Christiana*—was not published in his lifetime; it was not published until the more open-minded, free-thinking eighteenth century.

He died in November, 1674, a few months after the appearance of the second edition of *Paradise Lost.* He was sixty-six years old. The parish church, which he had not attended living, received him, dead. He was buried in St. Giles's Cripplegate, followed to the grave by a great crowd of neighbours, admirers and sympathisers.

48